SONGS
FOR SILENT
MOMENTS

Songs FOR SILENT moments

Prayers for Daily Living

Lois Walfrid Johnson

AUGSBURG Publishing House • Minneapolis

SONGS FOR SILENT MOMENTS

Scripture quotations unless otherwise noted are from Today's English Version of the Bible, copyright 1966, 1971, and 1976 by American Bible Society, and are used by permission.

Scripture quotations marked NIV are from the Holy Bible: New International Version. Copyright 1978 by the New York International Bible Society. Used by permission of Zondervan Bible Publishers.

Photos: H. Armstrong Roberts, 11. RNS, 21, 85, 106. Paul M. Schrock, 27, 56, 113. Mimi Forsyth, 30, 83. Eva Luoma, 34, 50, 97. Vivienne, 39. Lutheran Standard, 49, 59, 117. Philip Gendreau, 67. Camerique, 72. Paul S. Conklin, 90. Harold M. Lambert, 100.

To my parents,
Mom and Dad Walfrid,
who first taught me to pray

CONTENTS

PREFACE

Every one of us needs to have hope, whether we face daily frustrations and boredom or major crises. Those who have no hope find their will to live is gone, and Jesus Christ wants us to know just the opposite. "I have come in order that you might have life—life in all its fullness," he said (John 10:10).

That abundant life is available to you and to me in a relationship through prayer. Whether the day we face abounds in joy, sorrow, or somewhere in between makes no difference. Whether our problems are large or small does not matter. Circumstances seem big or little depending on our ability to cope and our willingness to rely on the Lord who wants to overcome for us.

Two months after doctors told me I had cancer a pair of Baltimore orioles flew into our yard. Never before nor since have we had orioles, and I speculated about their arrival, for it was late in the season. Yet as I watched their movements, my questioning changed to wonder. With a flash of orange feathers the male and his more somber-hued mate built their nest—two feet from the end of a pencil-thin elm branch and approximately 25 feet above the ground.

From my vantage point in the kitchen, I decided that among builders orioles rank as professionals. In a strong wind their completed nest tossed back and forth, yet remained safe. When the storm was over, the male flew to a nearby wire and began to sing.

Our Creator gave the orioles a special protection—their ability to build carefully and to rise above circumstances. During my first summer on chemotherapy their presence encouraged me. The pair seemed God's special gift, for I began to hope that I could also sing in spite of circumstances.

During those months I wrote *Either Way, I Win.* The prayers that follow are the practical expression of the suggestions for growth made in that book. Some of these prayers came out of the height of the storm; others developed as the storm subsided and God allowed me to know the freedom of song from the heart. Whatever the weather, I found that my experience of joy depended on two things—my willingness to build and my willingness to receive the Spirit's ongoing work in my life.

As I realized my private devotional time had even greater meaning than before, I started following a pattern I still continue. Frequently I begin by singing songs that ask the Holy Spirit to open my eyes, to give me understanding, to help me listen. At other times I simply pray, "Lord, what do you want me to know or understand?" Then I read a devotional book, carefully studying the verse it suggests by comparing it in more than one version or paraphrase. I also read verses that precede and follow so that I see a passage as a whole. Independent of this, I read through the Bible, taking a chapter or two each day. Surprisingly often, the key thoughts from the two sources correspond or supplement each other.

By making some verses seem to jump off the page, the Holy Spirit calls my attention to the message I be-

9

lieve he wants me to comprehend. As I take those insights seriously, he offers the conviction, comfort, or counsel that I need. I live the words of Oswald Chambers: "Our capacity in spiritual matters is measured by the promises of God."

Often my prayers flow spontaneously out of my reading of Scripture, and I have included in this book many of the promises most meaningful to me. My relationship with Jesus Christ is built on truth. It doesn't matter that my private prayers are frequently fragments or disconnected sentences. *The important thing is not how my phrases sound, but that I begin praying and allow the Holy Spirit to teach me.* The more I pray, the more I learn about how to pray. Though all around me changes and circumstances threaten to defeat me, I know that the Lord Jesus Christ never fails.

And so, these prayers are honest efforts to turn situations over to God. Whether you use them in a group or for personal devotions, ask the Holy Spirit to give life to the thoughts, to speak through them, offering faith. Ask him to provide promises and prayers at the right time, in such a way that they meet needs in your daily living.

I hope that these prayers will be only beginnings for your own spontaneous talks with God. Whether you are practiced or stumbling isn't important; prayer offers the opportunity to build carefully. Whatever your circumstance—happiness, frustration, or suffering—go forward in the excitement and the strength of a living relationship. Know that you are part of a choir in which countless others sing. May these prayers, these songs for silent moments, lead to the gift of the Spirit's hope.

SONGS OF *FAITH*

*To have faith is to be sure of the
things we hope for, to be certain
of the things we cannot see.*
Hebrews 11:1

*The word hope I take for faith;
and indeed hope is nothing else but
the constancy of faith.*
John Calvin

TEACH ME TO PRAY

O sing to the Lord a new song, for he has done marvelous things! His right hand and his holy arm have gotten him victory. . . . Make a joyful noise to the Lord, all the earth; break forth into joyous song and sing praises! (Ps. 98:1, 4 RSV)

As I look upward
to the wonder of your world,
you help me look beyond
the everydayness of my world.
Teach me to pray, Lord,
giving me the ability
to sing a new song—
not to avoid reality, but to cope
more effectively with it;
not to escape problems near-at-hand,
or cries heard from far away,
but as a means through which I grow
in my relationship with you.
Make me aware of your presence,
eager to discover your solutions
for people and for needs.
By the power of your Spirit
transform my prayers from daily living
into songs of faith in you.

REMIND ME

"Ask and it will be given to you; seek and you will find; knock and the door will be opened to you. For everyone who asks receives; he who seeks finds; and to him who knocks, the door will be opened. . . . If you, then, though you are evil, know how to give good gifts to your children, how much more will your Father in heaven give good gifts to those who ask him!" (Matt. 7:7-8, 11 NIV)

Someone has said,
"Your loved one
is just a prayer away."
Yet, Lord, how often I forget
how much you care
about that cherished one.
Do you grow impatient
of my worry,
simply waiting
for me to be obedient
and to ask?

ON THOSE DAYS

For this reason I fall on my knees before the
Father, from whom every family in heaven and on
earth receives its true name. I ask God from the
wealth of his glory to give you power through his
Spirit to be strong in your inner selves . . . .
(Eph. 3:14-16)

On those days
when everything goes wrong—
when someone tracks mud
across a newly-washed floor;
when my younger children cry
or the older ones fight;
when I have too much to do
and too little time to do it—
on those days
give me your strength.

If I long for miracles
and should be asking
for sustaining grace,
support me, Holy Spirit.
Replace my on-edge feeling
with a sense of humor
that allows me to smile
at myself first,
then leads to peace
in spite of circumstances.

CREATE IN ME

For it is by God's grace that you have been saved through faith. It is not the result of your own efforts, but God's gift, so that no one can boast about it (Eph. 2:8-9).

I *want* to believe,
I *want* to trust,
yet isn't even that feeling
a way of saying, "It's up to me—
I can do it by myself"?
Forgive me, Jesus,
when I sin by not believing,
when I forget that your salvation
and all your other gifts
really *are* your gifts.
Thank you for calling me,
for drawing me to yourself.
Create in me the hunger to seek,
the faith to believe,
the trust to receive.

NOW

*We beg you who have received God's grace not to
let it be wasted. Hear what God says: "When the
time came for me to show you favor, I heard you;
when the day arrived for me to save you, I helped
you." Listen! This is the hour to receive God's
favor; today is the day to be saved!* (2 Cor. 6:1-2)

Lord, how many times have I told you,
"Perhaps I'll be more ready next year"?
More ready to stop striving,
to make the leap of faith, believe?
To care for others or to grow?
To look at life, not through myself
or my abilities,
but with the knowledge
of your power and love?
When I am tempted to delay,
to think that next year is the time
to pray, believe, and grow,
remind me that the time is *now*.

BENEATH MY BEST

This happened in order to make come true what
the prophet had said:
"Tell the city of Zion,
Look, your king is coming to you!
He is humble and rides on a donkey
and on a colt, the foal of a donkey."
(Matt. 21:4-5)

How strange that you would come
in simple robe on humble beast
when I would come
in polished car and Sunday best.
Yet far beneath my outward best
lies all my pride,
and sometimes my hypocrisy,
my worship simply habit.
Lord, forgive!
Forgive my longing to be everything
that you with clearest insight
put aside.
Touch not my outer surface only,
but in my depths
create humility.

IN DEEP WATER

But God has shown us how much he loves us—it was
while we were still sinners that Christ died for
us! By his death we are now put right with God. . . .
For sin pays its wage—death; but God's free gift
is eternal life in union with Christ Jesus our
Lord (Rom: 5:8-9; 6:23).

Thank you, Jesus,
that as I struggle in deep water,
you reach out,
offering the life preserver
of your love
and your forgiveness.
Thank you that by dying on the cross
you made salvation a gift
for all who come to you.
I hear, I believe,
I receive.
Lord Jesus, I praise you
for eternal life
beginning this moment.
Thank you for saving me
from drowning.

FOR YOUR BLESSINGS

Praise the Lord!
Praise God in his sanctuary;
praise him in his mighty firmament!
Praise him for his mighty deeds;
praise him according to his exceeding greatness! . . .
Let everything that breathes praise the Lord!
Praise the Lord! (Ps. 150:1-2, 6 RSV)

Praise the Lord
for the bountiful blessings
he has showered upon me—
for giving me shelter
and the food and clothing I need;
for the richness of friends
and neighbors and family;
for good health,
or strength in the midst
of poor health.
Lord, I praise you!

ABILITY TO ENDURE

Blessed is the man who perseveres under trial, because when he has stood the test, he will receive the crown of life that God has promised to those who love him. When tempted, no one should say, "God is tempting me." For God cannot be tempted by evil, nor does he tempt anyone . . . .
(James 1:12-13 NIV)

When I fear the trials
that come to all people—
the tests that are part
of being alive—
remind me, Spirit of God,
that you provide the ability
to run the race of life.
I turn over to you
each one of my difficulties.
In the name of Jesus
I ask for protection
for my loved ones and me.
Thank you for giving
the ability to endure—faith
in spite of circumstances.
In faith I receive your crown,
your crown of victory!

FAITH, NOT FEELINGS

*But when you pray, you must believe and not doubt
at all. Whoever doubts is like a wave in the sea
that is driven and blown about by the wind. A person like that, unable to make up his mind and un-
decided in all he does, must not think that he
will receive anything from the Lord* (James 1:6-8).

At times I feel as inconsistent
as a wave in the sea,
driven and blown about by the wind.
Thank you that you have given me
the ability to feel,
to love, to know joy.
Yet teach me to live and pray by faith,
not being ruled by my feelings.
Give me the balance
between asking and thanking,
between confessing and receiving,
between learning with my mind
and praising with my spirit.
I rejoice, Holy Spirit,
that as I cooperate with you
your power enables me
to pray and live
with your consistency.

ONLY FOR ME

*"When, however, the Spirit comes, who reveals the
truth about God, he will lead you into all the
truth. He will not speak on his own authority,
but he will speak of what he hears and will tell
you of things to come. He will give me glory,
because he will take what I say and tell it to
you"* (John 16:13-14).

I praise you, Holy Spirit,
for the warm sense
of being taught by you.
Thank you for the moments
when you bring God's message alive,
as though it were written
or spoken only for me.
Thank you that when I turn
your promises into prayers
your Word becomes flesh
and dwells within me.

OPEN WINDOWS

And I will make them and the places round about my
hill a blessing; and I will cause the shower to come
down in its season; there shall be showers of
blessing (Ezek. 34:26 ASV).

As I pray for needs and changes
in the lives of others,
I become discouraged
and wonder if you are grieved.
Do you hurt inside as people
resist and say no,
slamming the windows
of their souls against you?
And do you grieve about me
when I hold out parts of myself,
not allowing you to reign
as Lord in my life?
Give me the willingness
to dwell close to you,
the faith to throw wide
the windows of my spirit.
I praise you, Lord!
With uplifted hands I receive
your showers of blessing.

BEYOND GOOD FRIDAY

I ask that your minds may be opened to see his light,
so that you will know what is the hope to which he
has called you, how rich are the wonderful blessings
he promises his people, and how very great is his
power at work in us who believe. This power working
in us is the same as the mighty strength which he
used when he raised Christ from death and seated
him at his right side in the heavenly world.
(Eph. 1:18-20)

Why do I dwell on the close-up
and the near-at-hand
like your followers
who stood beneath the cross,
sure they had lost all?
Lord Jesus, give me the grace—
the faith—
to look beyond the immediate,
believing
that in spite of what I see,
your power
is still available
for me.
Praise God! You are risen!

POSTSCRIPT

Humble yourselves, then, under God's mighty hand,
so that he will lift you up in his own good time.
Leave all your worries with him, because he cares
for you (1 Peter 5:6-7).

God, whenever I begin
worrying about my children
remind me
that you are their Father,
as well as their Creator,
and that you love them
even more than I do.

P.S.
And thank you
for loving parents
much more than parents
like themselves.

YOU ARE LORD!

*Through Jesus, therefore, let us continually offer
to God a sacrifice of praise—the fruit of lips that
confess his name* (Heb. 13:15 NIV).

*Let us, then, always offer praise to God as our sacrifice
through Jesus, which is the offering presented by lips
that confess him as Lord* (Heb. 13:15).

Lord, I delight myself in you!
Out of the joy welling from my depths
I bless your name.
I kneel before you in worship,
singing alleluia.
Let my praises be my sacrifice to you,
the outpouring of my life,
the offering of my faith.
Jesus, you are Lord!
I confess your name, your salvation.
I praise you for being *my* Lord!

TO THE SOURCE

Then Jesus told his disciples a parable to teach
them that they should always pray and never become
discouraged (Luke 18:1).

You know, Lord,
how often I pray about hurts,
trying to put bandages
on the wounds of others.
But I forget to pray
for the unthinking people
or the cruel circumstances
that caused the wounds.
Spirit of God,
give me the discernment
to recognize the sin
or the source of a problem.
Then supply me with the faith
to persistently intercede,
seeking to correct the basic wrong.
Thank you that when I have prayed enough
you give your release of peace.

YOUR MUSIC

Make a joyful noise to the Lord, all the lands!
Serve the Lord with gladness!
Come into his presence with singing!
Know that the Lord is God!
It is he that made us, and we are his.
(Ps. 100:1-3 RSV)

I will sing to the Lord as long as I live;
I will sing praise to my God while I have being.
(Ps. 104:33 RSV)

I praise you, Lord!
Your music is never-ending
in the songs
your creation plays—
a newborn's cry,
a puppy's whimper,
a soaring concerto,
a carefree flute,
a tumbling stream,
the splash of surf
against a rocky shore.
In the music of my spirit
give me a quietness of heart
that hears your still small voice
and worships you.

UPSIDE DOWN

"But whoever believes in him will not be dis-
appointed" (Rom. 9:33).

I was doing all right
learning to cross-country ski
until I became fearful and looked down
and that's when I fell.
How often I look down spiritually
and there's nothing there
except my feet and reasons to be afraid.
Help me look up, Jesus,
and the right distance ahead.
Thank you for laying out
the path before me, for breaking
that important first track.

ROADBLOCKS AHEAD

*"You will succeed, not by military might or by your
own strength, but by my spirit. Obstacles as great as
mountains will disappear before you. You will rebuild
the Temple, and as you put the last stone in place,
the people will shout, 'Beautiful, beautiful!' "*
(Zech. 4:6-7)

I'm facing roadblocks, Jesus,
obstacles that keep me from praying,
from growing in my relationship with you.
Forgive my sins, my fears, or doubts
that hide my view of your blessing—
your guidance for my life.
Help me to see those barriers
through your eternal perspective,
knowing when you're saying, "Wait,"
or when it's time to travel on.

In my impatience, Jesus,
give me your ability to wait;
increase my understanding of your purpose.
But give me your courage also,
that when it's time to move ahead
I'm willing to be led, following you.

HIDDEN PRAYER

"When you pray, go into your room, close the door and pray to your Father, who is unseen. Then your Father, who sees what is done in secret, will reward you" (Matt. 6:6 NIV).

For moments of joyful expectancy,
like fish leaping into the air at sundown,
I praise you, Father.
Thank you for a oneness with you—
a peace that enters my spirit and spreads,
like widening circles across a quiet lake.
Thank you that in those times
I sense that I'm alone with you.
Thank you for giving me the freedom
to pray whatever I want, knowing
it doesn't matter how my phrases sound.
I praise you, Father, that my reward
for hidden prayer often comes
as I wait and listen to you,
getting to know you better.

BECOMING ONE

"The glory which thou hast given me I have given to them, that they may be one even as we are one, I in them and thou in me, that they may become perfectly one, so that the world may know that thou hast sent me and hast loved them even as thou hast loved me."
(John 17:22-23 RSV)

Lord,
it's more than a surprise
whenever our family
discovers something
that all of us enjoy doing.
It's your miracle
of joining links in a chain.
Thank you that your Spirit
in our midst creates unity—
oneness in you.
May our love for each other
continue to grow, our love
for you welding us together—
individuals, yet one
in the family of God.

GO IN PEACE

She had heard about Jesus, so she came in the crowd behind him, saying to herself, "If I just touch his clothes, I will get well." She touched his cloak, and her bleeding stopped at once; and she had the feeling inside herself that she was healed of her trouble. . . . Jesus said to her, "My daughter, your faith has made you well. Go in peace, and be healed of your trouble" (Mark 5:27-29, 34).

Jesus,
whenever I feel
that physical wholeness
is an impossibility,
remind me of that woman
who believed,
then *knew*
she had been healed.
Help me to simply reach up,
touching your robe in faith.
I praise you, Jesus!
I go in peace.

AFTER THE DESERT

For this reason, ever since I heard of your faith in the Lord Jesus and your love for all of God's people, I have not stopped giving thanks to God for you. I remember you in my prayers and ask the God of our Lord Jesus Christ, the glorious Father, to give you the Spirit, who will make you wise and reveal God to you, so that you will know him (Eph. 1:15-17).

It had been a long spiritual dry spell
and I entered church without expectation.
Then you reminded me to pray,
"Alleluia, I praise you!"
and something within me changed;
instead of slumbering, I worshiped.
Thank you, Holy Spirit, for that oasis,
and for all your streams of water
encouraging me to believe.

SONGS OF
PROMISE

*Let us hold on firmly to the hope
we profess, because we can trust
God to keep his promise.*
Hebrews 10:23

*I believe that problems can be
dissolved by grace, like a mist
that is dissipated by the sunshine.
One sees the Christian Gospel of
salvation quite concretely at work
in the gradual dissolution of
tangled problems, without any of
them being solved in the usual
sense of the word.*
Paul Tournier
The Person Reborn

INTO LIGHT

Jesus said to him, "Have you believed because you
have seen me? Blessed are those who have not seen
and yet believe" (John 20:29 RSV).

Must I, like Thomas,
go out into the night
to stumble on a dusty street,
heartsick, afraid,
my darkness more than sun gone down?
Each time I wonder if he walked alone
I stagger through my questions, doubts,
until at last returning   .
to the locked but friend-filled room.
Still, Lord, you understood
the needs of Thomas,
and to me you say,
"See my nailprints? Touch my side."
Those costly words
and possible reopening of your wounds
teach me yet more of your compassion,
your willingness to offer gifts
of trust and faith.
My Lord, my God,
make me one of those
who, without sight, believe.

YOU FILL ME

"I have seen his ways, but I will heal him; I will guide him and restore comfort to him, creating praise on the lips of the mourners in Israel. Peace, peace, to those far and near," says the Lord. "And I will heal them" (Isa. 57:18-19 NIV).

Though I feel no alleluias in my heart,
teach me to open my lips and sing,
offering praises with my will.
Remind me that if I am willing to begin
you fill me with the faith,
the sense of all rightness, the healing,
and the peace I need.
Create in me the ability to trust,
to be complete in you.
I praise you, God the Father!
I praise you, God the Son!
I praise you, God the Holy Spirit!

ON YOUR FOUNDATION

*But each one must be careful how he builds. For
God has already placed Jesus Christ as the one and
only foundation, and no other foundation can be
laid. . . . And the quality of each person's work will be
seen when the Day of Christ exposes it.*
(1 Cor. 3:10-11, 13)

For the blessing and challenge of work,
I praise you, Lord!
Thank you for moments when things go well—
moments that give perspective
to the times of great frustration.
Transform my striving with the assurance
that if you want my work raised up
you will prosper it,
but if you want it to fail,
you can allow that also.
Help me to rest in that awareness,
realizing I am only expected to build well,
on the foundation of Jesus Christ.
Give me the courage to build with materials
that will survive the fire—
the gold of honesty, the silver of fairness,
the precious jewels of nothing
that needs to be hidden.
In your name I ask that you enable me
to do my best with the task
that is nearest at hand. Thank you!

AS YOU LOVE

There is no fear in love; perfect love drives out all fear. So then, love has not been made perfect in anyone who is afraid, because fear has to do with punishment. We love because God first loved us. (1 John 4:18-19)

Forgive me, Lord Jesus,
when my reactions to my children's behavior
spring from concern for myself, not them.
Thank you that it's not my reputation
as a parent that counts,
but whether my children become mature,
Christ-filled adults.
Create in me the faith to persist in prayer,
but also to recognize the point
at which they are responsible
for their own actions.

Help me remember I cannot be all things
to all people, not even with my own family.
Give my children the right friends—
ones who will lead them to you
or strengthen them in their Christian walk,
whichever is needed.

Remind me that I succeed as a parent
only by letting my children go,
relinquishing them completely to you.
By the power of your Spirit transform me,
giving your ability to forgive,
to stand by, and to love,
as you love those who seek your grace.

WITH A THANKFUL HEART

Have no anxiety about anything, but in everything
by prayer and supplication with thanksgiving let
your requests be made known to God (Phil. 4:6 RSV).

I used to think that being anxious
is a way of showing
that I care for someone,
yet that's not true, Lord, is it?
Isn't my worry really a lack of trust,
a failure to believe
that you *will work* in a situation?
Teach me to turn my concern
into something positive—
the motivation to pray.
Through the power of your Spirit
remind me of friends and loved ones,
acquaintances or strangers,
when they need immediate
or ongoing prayer.
Thank you that I don't have to know
all the details and circumstances—
that even as I pray
and thank you for the answers
you are already working
in everything.

HERE AM I

And he touched my mouth, and said: "Behold, this
has touched your lips; your guilt is taken away,
and your sin is forgiven." And I heard the voice of
the Lord saying, "Whom shall I send, and who will
go for us?" Then I said, "Here am I! Send me."
(Isa. 6:7-8 RSV)

I doubt if this is the day
that you should send me, Lord:
I'm really tired—what's more,
I don't *feel* like talking to neighbors,
friends, and all those you prepare.
Yet thank you that I can come to you,
speaking honestly, and you understand.
In these moments with you
make me aware of your holiness;
let me hear the shout
of "Holy, holy, holy is the Lord of hosts!"
Forgive me, Lord—make my lips,
my attitudes, my spirit clean.
Revitalize my energy, my faith, my thoughts,
that I respond with joy,
"Here am I! Send me!"

FEAR NOT

*Jesus said to her, "I am the resurrection and the life;
he who believes in me, though he die, yet shall he
live, and whoever lives and believes in me shall never
die. Do you believe this?"* (John 11:25-26 RSV)

The corridor is empty.
My footsteps echo
as I walk its length alone.
Why, God? Why?
Are you with me even now
in the aching pain of loss?
in the void that is my heart?
in the anger of my spirit?

Does this corridor lead anywhere?
Like your friends on Easter morning
I must reach the garden tomb.
Yet is everything that I believed in,
hoped for, and dreamed about
gone forever?

Is that you, God?
Are you speaking through your angels?
Are you saying, "Fear not. He is risen"?
Are you telling me the reason for my hope,
the reason for my faith—your Son—
is still alive?

YOU ARE WITH ME

*I have said this to you, that in me you may have
peace. In the world you have tribulation; but be of
good cheer, I have overcome the world.*
(John 16:33 RSV)

*I have told you these things so that in Me you
may have perfect peace* and *confidence. In the world
you have tribulation* and *trials* and *distress* and
*frustration; but be of good cheer—take courage, be
confident, certain, undaunted—for I have overcome
the world.—I have deprived it of power to harm,
have conquered it [for you]* (John 16:33 Amplified).

Thank you, Jesus,
that in the moment of crisis,
in the shock
and numbness of disbelief,
you are with me—
upholding, strengthening, loving,
cradling me like an infant
within your protecting arms.
Make me so conscious
of your ability to overcome
that even when
I cannot *feel* your presence,
I will *know* your promise of peace
shall not be removed.

EVERY TEAR

And he said, "These are they who have come out of the great tribulation; they have washed their robes and made them white in the blood of the Lamb. . . . Never again will they hunger; never again will they thirst. The sun will not beat upon them, nor any scorching heat. For the Lamb at the center of the throne will be their shepherd; he will lead them to springs of living water. And God will wipe away every tear from their eyes" (Rev. 7:14, 16-17 NIV).

Guard me, Lord, from tears that rise
from self-pity or self-centeredness,
yet teach me to be unembarrassed
by needed tears,
both my own and those of others.
Thank you that you created me
with the ability to cry,
and strange as it may sound,
thank you for the moments
when tears become a gift—
a spontaneous thank-you
for something meaningful,
a release from pent-up emotions,
or a way to express deep sorrow.
Thank you that one day
I will know a time
with neither hunger, nor thirst,
nor scorching heat—
a time when you will wipe away
my every tear. Praise God!

A NEW BEGINNING

*Blessed be the name of the Lord from this time forth
and for evermore! From the rising of the sun to its
setting the name of the Lord is to be praised!*
(Ps. 113:2-3 RSV)

Blessed be your name, Jesus!
I praise you for your times of renewal—
for quiet moments as the dawn is breaking.
I praise you for glimpses of light
coloring the eastern sky,
for the rumble of thunder,
the lightning of approaching storm.
When the clouds seem to threaten,
remind me that they are filled
with the rains of your promise.
Thank you that each day is a new beginning
and your beginnings have good endings.
Blessed be your name!

AFTER YOUR HEART

"And I will give you shepherds after my own heart,
who will feed you with knowledge and understanding."
(Jer. 3:15 RSV)

Lord God, you know our need
for shepherds with the ability to minister
to a variety of persons and situations.
You know our need for individuals
to speak words of life to us—
words founded on the salvation of Jesus Christ
and filled with the power of your Spirit.
In your name I ask
for shepherds after your own heart,
for spiritual leaders to guide us
with wisdom and understanding.
Thank you that already you have prepared
your persons for this time.

JOINED TO YOU

"If a family divides itself into groups which fight each other, that family will fall apart" (Mark 3:25).

Jesus, help my loved ones and me
not to separate ourselves
from each other,
forming islands in our ways of thinking,
in our ways of doing things.
Instead create in us
the willingness to continue learning
about each other and with each other.
Make us peninsulas, Jesus,
joined to you within our world.

TO REJOICE AGAIN

The wilderness and the dry land shall be glad,
the desert shall rejoice and blossom;
like the crocus it shall blossom abundantly,
and rejoice with joy and singing.
(Isa. 35:1-2 RSV)

Sometimes life seems like withered grass,
dried by hot summer winds.
Be with those who know that kind of sorrow,
who suffer separation through divorce or death.
I hold them up to you, Lord,
asking for your strength in loneliness,
your comfort in frustration and tears,
and your peace in spite of circumstances.
Help me to let them know that I care,
that I want to understand their needs.

Thank you Lord, that in the healing of time
your rains bring a new life.
Thank you that deeper than happiness
is the blossoming of your joy.

A LIFTING UP

Two are better than one, because they have a good
reward for their toil. For if they fall, one will lift
up his fellow; but woe to him who is alone when
he falls and has not another to lift him up.
(Eccles. 4:9-10 RSV)

All around me are people with needs—
needs so deep that only you
can meet and answer them.
Make me ready, Lord, fully aware
of where you want me to be
and when you want me to listen.
Yet do not allow my sympathy
to become a well-meaning
but false consolation
that hinders someone's response
to the conviction of your Spirit.
Give me your wisdom, your balance,
so that my help is a lifting up
that enables others to see you.

FOR THE SMILES

You yourselves are our letter, written on our hearts,
known and read by everybody. You show that you
are a letter from Christ, the result of our ministry,
written not with ink but with the Spirit of the living
God, not on tablets of stone but on tablets of human
hearts (2 Cor. 3:2-3 NIV).

For the smiles
of the people you created,
I praise you, Lord!
For a toddler's shout,
a young girl's laughter,
a 12-year old's hurrah,
a teenager's applause,
a bride's radiance,
a new parent's gleam,
a woman's glow,
a grandfather's chuckle.
For all your ways
of giving joy,
I praise you, Lord!
For the sparkle,
the zest you add to life,
I praise and worship you!

STRONG ENOUGH TO STAND

*"And the rain fell, and the floods came, and the winds
blew and beat upon that house, but it did not fall,
because it had been founded on the rock."*
(Matt. 7:25 RSV)

Sometimes I need to ask,
Am I doing all that I can
to make our marriage healthy?
Together we wonder,
Are we building upon the rock
or upon the sand?
When our marriage is good,
give us gratefulness and humility, Lord.
Give us also the power to cope
with the big and the little storms
tearing husband and wife apart.
Fill us with an even greater love;
in an unfaithful world
keep us faithful to each other.
Protect us against all that interferes
with your will for unity and joy
in our relationship.
Thank you for being our master carpenter;
show us how to build a home
strong enough to stand.

THE MUD OF WORDS

Likewise the Spirit helps us in our weakness; for
we do not know how to pray as we ought, but the
Spirit himself intercedes for us with sighs too deep
for words. And he who searches the hearts of men
knows what is the mind of the Spirit, because the
Spirit intercedes for the saints according to the will
of God (Rom. 8:26-27 RSV).

When I bog down
in the mud of words—
seeking to frame a prayer
in exactly the right way,
or in trying to understand
your best will and purpose—
remind me, Holy Spirit,
to turn the whole situation
over to you.
Set me on firm ground;
pray through me,
bypassing my mind,
to intercede
in the best way possible.

YOUR KINGDOM FIRST

Bring the full amount of your tithes to the Temple,
so that there will be plenty of food there. Put me to
the test and you will see that I will open the windows
of heaven and pour out on you in abundance all
kinds of good things. I will not let insects destroy
your crops, and your grapevines will be loaded with
grapes (Mal. 3:10-11).

When our money doesn't seem
to stretch far enough
remind me, Lord, if there are things
I have failed to do.
Have I given you the first portion
of all that I have?
Have I shared my material blessings
with those who have helped me spiritually?
Create in me the ability to spend less,
knowing the difference between needs and wants,
but remind me also of my priorities.
Thank you that you can give me
your ability to seek the kingdom first.

HARMFUL HABITS

For it is God who works in you to will and to act
according to his good purpose (Phil. 2:13 NIV).

You created me, God, and you know me
better than I know myself.
Unfortunately, you also know my bad habits.
But you gave me my will;
in this moment I give it back to you,
surrendering myself completely
in asking for the help I need.
In your name, Jesus, I *will* to be willing
to overcome habits that are harmful to me.
Heal the original insecurities
that caused me to begin those patterns.
Work in me, bringing needed changes
in my mind, emotions, body, and spirit.
Give me a distaste for those things
you do not want me to have.
Thank you, Holy Spirit, that as I cooperate
with you, your power gives me the victory.
Thank you that I will live in your freedom,
that already you are working within me.
Praise God! In faith I receive!

BREAD FOR THE HUNGRY

As the rain and snow
come down from heaven,
and do not return to it
without watering the earth
and making it bud and flourish,
so that it yields seed for the sower
and bread for the eater,
so is my word that goes out from my mouth:
It will not return to me empty,
but will accomplish what I desire
and achieve the purpose for which I sent it.
(Isa. 55:10-11 NIV)

I thought I was following
the leading of your Spirit, Lord,
but it seems as though
all that I had hoped for
and prayed about before witnessing
to that person did not happen.
Yet you promised you will not allow
your word to return empty,
that it waters the earth,
making it flourish. Thank you
that I can cling to that promise,
knowing I have been obedient
in sowing the seed.
Use the words you gave me
as bread for the hungry,
accomplishing your purpose
in your own time,
in whatever way is needful.

RAYS OF LOVE

Then Jonathan said to David. . . . "But show me
unfailing kindness like that of the Lord as long as I
live, so that I may not be killed, and do not ever
cut off your kindness from my family". . . . And
Jonathon had David reaffirm his oath out of love for
him, because he loved him as he loved himself.
(1 Sam. 20:12, 14-15, 17 NIV)

The other day I heard
someone describing a friend—
"Just like the sun makes me warm,
that's what he does for me."
Thank you, Father, for giving me
neighbors and friends
that do the same—
for using them as beams of light
revealing your grace and forgiveness.
I praise you for making them rays
of love that warm the earth and me.
When they need encouragement,
fill me with the same awareness,
the same willingness to help.

NO LONGER ALONE

*The Lord said to his people, "Stand at the crossroads
and look. Ask for the ancient paths and where the
best road is. Walk in it, and you will live in
peace"* (Jer. 6:16).

Strange, Lord,
I thought I had to walk alone
against the driving snow
of pain, discouragement—
yet alleluia!
Even as I felt
the cold bite of winter
you were there—
warming me, guiding me
with your presence.

GOOD NIGHT, LORD

In peace I will both lie down and sleep; for thou alone, O Lord, makest me dwell in safety.
(Ps. 4:8 RSV)

Lord, I put myself
and my world
into your gentle keeping.
Thank you
that you want me to rest.
Give me the ability
to lie down,
leaving my thoughts,
my anxieties,
my hopes,
and my dreams
in your competent hands.
Thank you that tomorrow
is soon enough
to begin caring again.
Good night, Lord.

SONGS OF CHALLENGE

Why are you downcast, O my soul?
Why so disturbed within me?
Put your hope in God,
for I will yet praise him,
my Savior and my God.
Psalm 42:11 NIV

When the darkness of dismay comes,
endure until it is over, because
out of it will come that following
of Jesus which is an unspeakable joy.
Oswald Chambers
My Utmost for His Highest

DAILY RESPONSE

*And in the morning, a great while before day, he rose
and went out to a lonely place, and there he prayed.*
(Mark 1:35 RSV)

Sorry, Jesus,
but I don't feel like praying today,
nor even like searching out the lonely place.
Yet while it was still dark
you found quietness and freedom
from the crowds who sought your power.
In those moments with your Father
you received new strength.

Forgive me, Jesus, when I feel
that prayer is "doing something."
Give me the faith to simply talk with you,
to learn the overcoming power that develops
in a relationship through prayer.
Create in me a hunger for Scripture,
that our conversations flow spontaneously
out of my reading of your Word.
Then, like the washing of the earth
by nighttime rains, bring me to life again,
to walk joyfully into your sunrise.

THE EVERYDAYS

Do you not know?
Have you not heard?
The Lord is the everlasting God,
the Creator of the ends of the earth.
He will not grow tired or weary,
and his understanding no one can fathom.
He gives strength to the weary
and increases the power of the weak.
Even youths grow tired and weary,
and young men stumble and fall;
but those who hope in the Lord
will renew their strength.
They will soar on wings like eagles;
they will run and not grow weary,
they will walk and not be faint.
(Isa. 40:28-31 NIV)

Always I think I need
strength for the crisis moments,
but so much more do I require
faith for the everydays.
When the dust on my furniture
seems like dust on my life,
clean up my discouragement,
polish my ability to know joy.
Thank you, Lord! I praise you!
I sense your arms around me.

THE FRUIT I NEED

But the Spirit produces love, joy, peace, patience, kindness, goodness, faithfulness, humility, and self-control. There is no law against such things as these. And those who belong to Christ Jesus have put to death their human nature with all its passions and desires. The Spirit has given us life; he must also control our lives (Gal. 5:22-25).

Holy Spirit, you know
that not all of my relationships
are what I'd like.
When I want to cry out in frustration,
use my irritating experiences—
my seemingly hopeless circumstances—
to develop in me patience and joy,
kindness, faithfulness, and self-control.
In those moments give me the willingness
to be controlled by you,
that you may produce the fruit I need.
Put to death my striving nature,
bringing alive my cooperation.
I praise you for creating a miracle—
for creating the love within!

IF I ABIDE

"If you abide in me, and my words abide in you, ask
whatever you will, and it shall be done for you."
(John 15:7 RSV)

Your promise,
"Whatever you ask in my name,"
is the foundation for miracles.
Yet so often I forget the condition,
"If you remain in me."
Graft me into your vine, Jesus—
teach me to abide,
that a continual turning to you
becomes a natural part of my life.
Give me an understanding
of your will and purpose,
and of how you want me to pray.
I praise you that in your name
I receive miracles,
because you have given me
the boldness to ask.

MOST OF ALL

So faith, hope, love abide, these three; but the greatest of these is love (1 Cor. 13:13 RSV).

It's easy, Lord,
to take my parents for granted.
If I walk in blindness,
create in me the ability
to see and meet their needs.
If I am deaf, help me to hear
and respond to their fears.
I thank you, Lord, for enriching
their lives with opportunities
to be useful, make friends,
and share laughter.
If illness or aging changes them,
show me how to receive
their requests with understanding—
not feeling guilty
for things I cannot do.
As they held my hand as a child,
enable me to give my support,
and most of all, my love.

ONGOING CREATIONS

They will be my people, and I will be their God. . . .
I will make an everlasting covenant with them: I will
never stop doing good to them, and I will inspire
them to fear me, so that they will never turn away
from me. I will rejoice in doing them good and will
assuredly plant them in this land with all my heart
and soul (Jer. 32:38, 40-41 NIV).

Praise God for his shaping of life
through anniversaries—
celebrations numbering years spent
or, if happily, years gained;
celebrations of small moments
that seem large because of meaning.

For outward, easily-seen anniversaries,
thank you, God, and thank you also
for the less visible ones—
for that sudden sense of wonder
when I stretched up, instead of
bending down to kiss my son;
for that first time after surgery
when I climbed a steep hill,
and found I was not panting.

Thank you for all of those ah! moments
in your ongoing creations of joy.
I praise you, God,
for making each person's anniversaries
unique happenings, gifts of love from you.

VERY CAREFULLY

The attitude you should have is the one that
Christ Jesus had:
He always had the nature of God,
but he did not think that by force he
should try to become equal with God.
Instead of this, of his own free will
he gave up all he had,
and took the nature of a servant.
(Phil. 2:5-8)

You know that I believe,
yet how often I believe very carefully,
making sure my "religion"
falls within the boundaries I have set.
Is that what's wrong, Jesus,
that I'm the one making the rules,
deciding the limits,
rather than yielding myself to you?

Forgive my pride,
my insistence on being in control.
Remove my rigidness and the excuses
I use instead of following you
without reservation.
Fill me with your nature.
Thank you that as you empower me
with your Spirit,
I learn the freedom
of surrendering all to you.
I praise you, Jesus!
I praise your holy name!

DISAPPOINTMENT

Fear not, for I am with you,
be not dismayed, for I am your God;
I will strengthen you, I will help you,
I will uphold you with my victorious right hand.
(Isa. 41:10 RSV)

In those moments
when I want to weep
and cannot,
give me the willingness—
even more,
the grace and courage—
to forgive
and then to love
those who have hurt me.

ACHIEVEMENT

There is nothing in us that allows us to claim that we are capable of doing this work. The capacity we have comes from God; it is he who made us capable of serving the new covenant, which consists not of a written law but of the Spirit. The written law brings death, but the Spirit gives life (2 Cor. 3:5-6).

Thank you for giving me
the drive and the need to achieve.
When I would do second best
where first best is needed,
remind me, Lord, that the way I work
reveals what I believe about you.
But help me also
when my sense of responsibility
tips out of balance,
becoming selfishness, misguided ambition,
or trampling on the feelings of others.
When I take myself or my work too seriously,
give me a sense of humor
and the ability to see myself in perspective.
I give you my willful striving,
even my feelings of competence,
when they hinder me from waiting
for your leading and your timing.
Thank you that when you give me your attitudes,
you are able to anoint my work,
to bless and prosper it.

THE WAY I AM

The Lord your God is with you,
he is mighty to save.
He will take great delight in you,
he will quiet you with his love,
he will rejoice over you with singing.
(Zeph. 3:17 NIV)

When I become too busy,
give me the opportunity
to just be me,
to enjoy the simple
yet astounding
things of life—
a chicken
pecking out of its shell,
a butterfly
from its cocoon,
a new leaf
unfurling in spring.
I praise you
that when I watch
new life emerge
you give
new life to me.

WHEN I AM DEPRESSED

Jesus said to them again, "Peace be with you. As the Father has sent me, even so I send you." And when he had said this, he breathed on them, and said to them, "Receive the Holy Spirit. If you forgive the sins of any, they are forgiven; if you retain the sins of any, they are retained" (John 20:21-23 RSV).

Yes, Jesus, it's true
that when I fail to forgive
I retain those sins within me.
When I am depressed,
give me the ability
to talk about my needs
and to realize why I am angry.
Help me deal with and set right
whatever is creating a problem.
I accept responsibility
for my share of that problem
and ask you to *forgive me*.
In your name, Jesus,
and by the power of your Spirit,
I forgive and ask you to bless
the individual or persons
who are involved.
I praise you that as I forgive
you speak to my mind,
my emotions, and my spirit,
bringing your deep wholeness
and peace. Thank you!

YOUR DWELLING PLACE

How lovely is thy dwelling place, O Lord of hosts!
(Ps. 84:1 RSV)

"How lovely is your dwelling place,"
the psalmist sang,
and as someone reminded me,
I, too, am your dwelling place—
a bit worn, in need of paint,
at best, imperfect—
but yes, Lord, your dwelling place.
How lovely, how beautiful
you make me
because you live within!

EACH OF MY GOINGS

Having gifts that differ according to the grace given us, let us use them: if prophecy, in proportion to our faith; if service, in our serving; he who teaches, in his teaching; he who exhorts, in his exhortation; he who contributes, in liberality; he who gives aid, with zeal; he who does acts of mercy, with cheerfulness.
(Rom. 12:6-8 RSV)

Spirit of God,
when I feel torn in every direction
because of activities I have chosen
or through demands others make on my time,
make me aware of the spiritual gift
or gifts in which you motivate me to serve.
Confirm those gifts to me
through the responses of others
and through the joy of fulfillment.
Thank you that when I work in an area
of your giftedness, I experience energy,
singleness of purpose, and unity of thought.
Make each of your sendings, each of my goings,
a holy thing, blessed and used by you.

FOR OUR FAMILY

And their people will say, "Let us go up the hill of the Lord, to the Temple of Israel's God. For he will teach us what he wants us to do; we will walk in the paths he has chosen" (Mic. 4:2).

Creator of families,
we ask you to give our family
the ability to grow in friendship and love.
Provide us with the quantity of time needed
to lay a foundation for moments of quality—
moments of deep, thoughtful sharing,
but also of fun and laughter.
Enrich our lives with the knowledge
that we can depend on one another
in both good times and difficult.
Help each of us to live in such a way
that we are worthy of trust.
Thank you, God. We praise you!

BEAMS OF GRACE

*God is light; in him there is no darkness at all. If
we claim to have fellowship with him yet walk in the
darkness, we lie and do not live by the truth. But if we
walk in the light, as he is in the light, we have
fellowship with one another, and the blood of Jesus,
his Son, purifies us from every sin* (1 John 1:5-7 NIV).

It seemed impossible,
but you did it again!
For moments of sunlight
that are beams of grace
in my life or the lives of others,
I praise you, Spirit of God!
For miracles I pray for
and yet forget to expect,
I praise you!
For the joy of a new Christian,
for evidence that you have worked
in that life, I praise you!
For your glow in a believer,
for your continuing growth,
I praise you!
I rejoice in your light;
I praise you!

WHEN I TRAVEL

A teacher of the Law came to him. "Teacher," he said, "I am ready to go with you wherever you go." Jesus answered him, "Foxes have holes, and birds have nests, but the Son of Man has no place to lie down and rest" (Matt. 8:19-20).

Thank you for the opportunity to travel,
to meet interesting people
and expand my horizons.
Protect the loved ones I leave behind
and wherever I go, Jesus, protect me.
But also use me for good,
putting me next to persons I can help.
Make my traveling yet another opportunity
to recognize the leading of your Spirit.
Thank you for giving me something
you did not have—a place of my own.
I praise you for that welcome moment
after every airport looks the same—
that heartwarming feeling of coming home.

GOOD NEWS

How beautiful on the mountains
are the feet of those who bring good news,
who proclaim peace,
who bring good tidings,
who proclaim salvation,
who say to Zion,
"Your God reigns!" (Isa. 52:7 NIV)

Lord, how often I am the bearer
of only bad news. I come to you
with the illness of this individual
or with the heartbreak of that person,
knowing you are glad to receive their hurts
and willingly shoulder them.
Yet through the power of your Spirit
teach me to also bring good tidings—
tidings that proclaim, "My God reigns!"
to those around me and to you.
Lord, give me the ability to see,
to understand, and to help
with that which is painful;
but give me the strength that comes
from crossing the mountains,
concentrating on good news.

LOOKING BACK

But the Lord says, "Do not cling to events of the past or dwell on what happened long ago. Watch for the new thing I am going to do. It is happening already—you can see it now! I will make a road through the wilderness and give you streams of water there. (Isa. 43:18-19)

There is therefore now no condemnation for those who are in Christ Jesus (Rom. 8:1 RSV).

Too often I dwell on the if onlys—
if only I had done this,
if only I had done that.
Teach me, Jesus, to know the difference
between conviction of your Spirit
and condemnation from the evil one.
I put the past that cannot be changed
into your hands; make a road
through the wilderness of my regret.
Forgive the things I've done wrong
and work in the places
where I've made mistakes,
using even my mistakes for your good.
I praise you, Jesus,
that with your forgiveness comes peace.
I praise you for the anticipation
you give as I move ahead
into your irresistible future.

A ONCE-GLOWING LOVE

"And now I give you a new commandment: love one another. As I have loved you, so you must love one another. If you have love for one another then everyone will know that you are my disciples."
(John 13:34-35)

When my love burns low
like a fire left untended,
remind me, Jesus,
that you commanded, "Love!"
Let not my smoldering withdrawal
extinguish friendship—
let not my failure to communicate
how I think and feel
become the dying embers
of a once-glowing love.

PACKAGED WITH CARE

*Do you not know that your body is a temple of the
Holy Spirit, who is in you, whom you have received
from God? You are not your own; you were bought
at a price. Therefore honor God with your body.*
(1 Cor. 6:19-20 NIV)

For the health and energy
to enjoy sports, thank you, Lord!
I praise you for the sun on my back
and the wind in my face.
I praise you for how good my body feels
after being active—
as I bike for several miles
or hit a long drive down the fairway,
as I swim, or jog, or hike, or ski.
Forgive me, Lord, whenever I take
good health for granted;
help me to regard it as a gift
and to handle with care
the package you have given me.
Thank you that the ability to join
in each activity is a way of saying,
"Praise you, Lord, I am well!"

ANGER

*May the God who gives us peace make you holy in
every way and keep your whole being—spirit, soul,
and body—free from every fault at the coming of our
Lord Jesus Christ. He who calls you will do it, because
he is faithful* (1 Thess. 5:23-24).

In those moments when my anger
becomes a teakettle
ready to boil over,
put me on simmer, Lord.
Cool me down
and teach me to wait
before pouring myself out
in front of others.

DOORMAT FAITH

*For this reason I remind you to keep alive the gift
that God gave you when I laid my hands on you. For
the Spirit that God has given us does not make us
timid; instead, his Spirit fills us with power, love, and
self-control* (2 Tim. 1:6-7).

Too often
I have doormat faith—
close to the entrance
of your church,
yet the kind of faith
that I can step on,
or over, or disregard,
if it should not be needed.
Lord, forgive!
Transform me, that instead
of stepping on
or over my beliefs,
empowered by your Spirit
I step out,
in faith that knows the urgency
of boldly overcoming
in your name.

FOR VACATIONS

*"Come to me, all who labor and are heavy laden, and
I will give you rest. Take my yoke upon you, and
learn from me; for I am gentle and lowly in heart,
and you will find rest for your souls. For my yoke is
easy, and my burden is light"* (Matt. 11:28-30 RSV).

Praise the Lord
for vacations large and small—
for weeks of relaxation
or minutes away from the phone;
for elaborate, far-flung trips
or walks around the block;
for moments of being active
or times of sitting still.
When I need rest, Lord,
give me the ability to take it,
to know that your arms
are always open to receive me.
Thank you that your rest means peace,
serenity within.
I praise you for creating
this time apart—
this vacation for me!

WHEN EVERYTHING GOES WELL

A voice cries:
"In the wilderness prepare the way of the Lord,
make straight in the desert a highway for our God.
Every valley shall be lifted up,
and every mountain and hill be made low;
the uneven ground shall become level,
and the rough places a plain" (Isa. 40:3-4 RSV).

In the wilderness
I longed for your highway—
your lifting of valleys,
your lowering of mountains.
Yet on the bumpy stretches
I sensed my limitations
and knew my need of you.
When the road becomes smooth,
I'm almost afraid, Lord,
for it was in the valley
that I learned your strength.
In the moments when everything
goes well, protect me.
Give me the stability of spirit
that welcomes a smooth road,
but continues to walk
side by side with you.

PRAISE THE LORD!

Bless the Lord, O my soul;
and all that is within me,
bless his holy name!
Bless the Lord, O my soul,
and forget not all his benefits,
who forgives all your iniquity,
who heals all your diseases (Ps. 103:1-3 RSV).

Praise the Lord!
Let all that is within me
praise his holy name!
Praise him for the splendor
of the reds and golds
of autumn.
Praise him for clouds of promise
that scud across the sky.
Praise him for wild grasses
blowing in the wind.
Praise him for his forgiveness,
and for his everlasting mercy.
Praise him for giving wholeness
of body, soul, and spirit.
Praise him for his love
and laughter,
and for the morning
that comes after tears.
Let all that is within me
remember and praise the Lord!

SONGS OF COURAGE

"For I know the plans I have for you," declares the Lord, "plans to prosper you and not to harm you, plans to give you hope and a future. Then you will call upon me and come and pray to me, and I will listen to you.
Jeremiah 29:11 NIV

When God gives you a word put it into practice without delay. The Word of God becomes flesh in our lives by our obedience to doing it.
Sister Albertine von Ufford

FOR EVERYTHING A SEASON

*There is a time for everything, and a season for every
activity under heaven. . . . He has made everything
beautiful in its time. He has also set eternity in the
hearts of men; yet they cannot fathom what God has
done from beginning to end* (Eccles. 3:1, 11 NIV).

When everything
seems sticky fingers
and smudges on the wall,
or when everyone
has left the nest
and all seems loneliness,
create in me deep gratitude
for your changing seasons of life.
Whether I belong to spring
or summer, autumn, winter,
keep me, Lord,
from longing for the past
or for distant years ahead.
I praise you for the present,
knowing you have brought me here.
Thank you for giving me
an acceptance of myself,
a trust in you,
that offers serenity and joy
whatever my season of life.

A FOOL FOR YOU

For Christ's sake we are fools; but you are wise in union with Christ! We are weak, but you are strong! We are despised, but you are honored! . . . For the Kingdom of God is not a matter of words but of power (1 Cor. 4:10, 20).

Give me your joyful glow, Lord!
Guard me against defensiveness
and the need to justify myself,
so I don't offend unnecessarily
those who surround me daily.
Yet when others criticize me
because of the way I believe in you,
remind me that your kingdom
is not a matter of words,
but of resurrection power.
Fill me with the faith and courage
to live the knowledge
that I am called to be a fool,
yet wise in you.
Amen, Lord Jesus. Alleluia!

MAKE ME A TREE

"Blessed is the man who trusts in the Lord,
whose trust is the Lord.
He is like a tree planted by water,
that sends out its roots by the stream,
and does not fear when heat comes,
for its leaves remain green,
and is not anxious in the year of drought,
for it does not cease to bear fruit."
(Jer. 17:7-8 RSV)

Make me a tree, Lord—
strong, thriving,
reaching for the light;
able to withstand the heat
because my roots are deep in you.
Keep my leaves green
and flourishing,
ready to shelter
those who come this way.
May the wind of your Spirit
produce fruit of love and joy,
kindness, goodness, peace,
for others to receive.

SEARCH FOR SPOTLIGHTS

John answered, "No one can have anything unless
God gives it to him. . . . He must become more
important while I become less important.
(John 3:27, 30)

Forgive me, Jesus,
when I search for spotlights,
wanting to rush ahead
to the well-publicized places
where everyone can see.
Give me John's willingness
to be less important,
to seek *your* glory first.
Through the power of your Spirit
train me in the small things—
in the day-to-day relying on you—
so I am ready
for larger responsibilities
if you want to give them
to me.

THE UNSEEN

*For this slight momentary affliction is preparing
for us an eternal weight of glory beyond all
comparison, because we look not to the things that
are seen but to the things that are unseen; for the
things that are seen are transient, but the things that
are unseen are eternal* (2 Cor. 4:17-18 RSV).

Each time I think
I've learned to handle hurt
I find I'm facing even deeper need,
and somehow all the learning
that has gone before
no longer is enough,
except perhaps—
do I turn more quickly
from myself,
my self-sufficiency,
to you?
Give me your strength, Lord.
I need it.

IF MY CUP

"You don't know what you are asking for," Jesus
answered the sons. "Can you drink the cup of
suffering that I am about to drink?" "We can," they
answered. "You will indeed drink from my cup,"
Jesus told them . . . (Matt. 20:22-23).

Thank you, Lord,
for the words of Oswald Chambers:
"If God has made your cup sweet,
drink it with grace;
if He has made it bitter,
drink it in communion with Him."
If my cup holds happiness, Lord,
guard me against insensitivity
or self-satisfaction,
yet do not allow me
to feel guilty for experiencing joy.
If suffering fills my life,
keep me from self-pity and bitterness.
Empower me to drink that cup
in communion with you.

YOUR JOY, MY STRENGTH

No temptation has overtaken you that is not common
to man. God is faithful, and he will not let you be
tempted beyond your strength, but with the
temptation will also provide the way of escape, that
you may be able to endure it (1 Cor. 10:13 RSV).

Thank you, Holy Spirit,
for giving me the understanding
that a temptation is anything
which threatens God's life within me.
Thank you that as you give me power,
testing does not weaken my faith,
but strengthens it.
Use my experiences in the wilderness
as you used Christ's temptations,
as preparation for ministry to others.

Guard my loved ones and me
against the evil one;
transform his harassment into good,
creating in me maturity
and unconditional trust.
Thank you that you will not allow me
to be tested
beyond my ability to remain firm.
I praise you for making
your joy, my strength.

WHEREVER I AM

I lift up my eyes to the hills.
From whence does my help come?
My help comes from the Lord,
who made heaven and earth.
He will not let your foot be moved,
he who keeps you will not slumber.
Behold, he who keeps Israel
will neither slumber nor sleep.
(Ps. 121:1-4 RSV)

I worship you, Lord!
I praise you that wherever I am
you lift my sight—
to the mountain peak,
the desert flower,
the grain-filled field,
or the backyard oak.
I praise you that in the city
or in the country,
in the apartment,
the big house or the little,
you are the Lord
of heaven and earth.
I praise you
for being you
and for all that you mean
to me.

EARTHEN VESSELS

"Woe to him who strives with his Maker,
an earthen vessel with the potter!
Does the clay say to him who fashions it,
'What are you making'?
or 'Your work has no handles'?" (Isa. 45:9-10 RSV).

Yet we who have this spiritual treasure are like
common clay pots, in order to show that the supreme
power belongs to God, not to us (2 Cor. 4:7).

As I realize you are allowing
suffering and disillusionment
to enter my life,
I struggle and protest, Lord,
trying to avoid your molding.
Yet am I, the clay, saying to you
who fashions me,
"What are you making?"

When I complain,
longing to escape—
to avoid the beauty
you would give me,
help me to sense the care
with which you shape me.
Remind me yet again
that you are my Maker
and by passing through the fire
I become an earthen vessel
you can use.

IN WEAKNESS

But he said to me, "My grace is sufficient for you, for my power is made perfect in weakness." I will all the more gladly boast of my weaknesses, that the power of Christ may rest upon me. For the sake of Christ, then, I am content with weaknesses, insults, hardships, persecutions, and calamities; for when I am weak, then I am strong (2 Cor. 12:9-10 RSV).

Lord,
when I wonder
if I have anything
to offer others,
use the awareness
of my weakness
to create in me
your gift
of compassion.
Thank you
that your power
rests on me.
I praise you
that when I am weak,
then I am strong.

SKILLFUL GARDENERS

He helps us in all our troubles, so that we are able to
help others who have all kinds of troubles, using the
same help that we ourselves have received from God.
Just as we have a share in Christ's many sufferings, so
also through Christ we share in God's great
help (2 Cor. 1:4-5).

Thank you for people who understand,
who like skillful gardeners
offer the water of listening
without judging, and caring
without smothering.
I praise you, Lord—
for giving them the ability
to see things clearly,
for creating in them a willingness
to help me separate
the weeds of my life
from the roots of my growth.
Give *me* the willingness to change
the parts of me that need changing
and then to share with gentleness
the help you have given me.

FROM YOUR HANDS

What is man that thou art mindful of him,
and the son of man that thou dost care for him?
Yet thou hast made him little less than God,
and dost crown him with glory and honor.
Thou hast given him dominion over the works of thy
*   hands;*
thou hast put all things under his feet.
(Ps. 8:4-6 RSV)

In the times I encounter shortages
give me courage, Lord.
Take away my feelings of panic
about the future.
Yet as one to whom you have given
dominion over the earth,
teach me to conserve,
preparing wisely for the time ahead.
Thank you that as I share
your gifts of flour and oil
you provide for me as you did
for the widow who fed Elijah—
multiplying whatever I have.
I rejoice that in plenty or in want
every blessing comes from your hands—
hands cupped and filled to overflowing
with your care and love.

SCHOOL OF YOUR MAKING

Now when they saw the boldness of Peter and John,
and perceived that they were uneducated, common
men, they wondered; and they recognized that they
had been with Jesus (Acts 4:13 RSV).

Now and then, Jesus,
you send me to schools of your making,
and last night was one of those moments.
As that visitor spoke, excited
about what you are doing in his life,
he was unschooled, unlearned, yet so very wise
in all that you had taught him.
I thought of Peter after Pentecost—
unafraid, unashamed, unhampered
by all he did not know.

When my education, or my lack of it,
gets in the way of my witness of you,
forgive me, Jesus.
Keep me always ready to learn,
but aware that I will never know enough,
that every word I utter
needs you as its source.
Speak through me that others may know
I have been with you.

FOR OUR LEADERS

I urge that petitions, prayers, requests, and thanks-
givings be offered to God for all people; for kings and
all others who are in authority . . . (1 Tim. 2:1-2).

Lord of our nation,
be with our political leaders,
that in the aloneness of their task
they may sense your strength.
When they are beset by problems
and the striving of persons and nations,
fill them with your peace. Make them aware
that you care for them as individuals,
that you offer guidance always accessible
and lift burdens too heavy to carry.

Give us leaders worthy of trust, Lord—
persons of integrity able to surround themselves
with individuals who discern the truth
and act courageously upon it.
Keep them conscious that they are servants
not of wealth, nor of fame, nor of position,
but of the good of all people.

Protect our leaders, that the complexities
of their positions do not blind them
to the needs of their families—
that out of the wholeness of their lives
they find strength for their responsibilities.
As they walk daily in your will,
give them your blessing, your wisdom,
your vision of justice, and your love.

113

DAY OF COMPLETION

And I am sure that he who began a good work in you
will bring it to completion at the day of Jesus
Christ (Phil. 1:6 RSV).

You began a good work, God,
in the moments in which
my children were conceived
or when they became mine
through adoption.
Whatever their age—
whether infants or toddlers,
pre-teens or young adults—
give me the faith to believe
that when you begin a good work
you bring it to the day of completion.

I FEEL LONELY, LORD

"I tell you the truth," Jesus said to them, "no one who
has left home or wife or brothers or parents or
children for the sake of the kingdom of God will fail
to receive many times as much in this age and, in
the age to come, eternal life" (Luke 18:29-30 NIV).

At times I feel lonely, Lord—
after moving to a strange city,
or because I've hesitated
in making new friends.
Yet there are other moments
and circumstances I cannot control.
Be near me when I experience aloneness
in the midst of a crowd
because I want to follow
after you unconditionally.
Help me to recognize your people,
to become complete in you
because I receive the love
and Christian fellowship I need.
Thank you, Jesus, that you have made real
your call to the kingdom.
I rejoice that you have promised
abundance of life even now.

LIFT MY HORIZONS

"I do not ask you to take them out of the world, but
I do ask you to keep them safe from the Evil One.
Just as I do not belong to the world, they do not
belong to the world. Dedicate them to yourself by
means of the truth; your word is truth. I sent them into
the world, just as you sent me into the world."
(John 17:15-18)

Jesus, when I want to avoid seeing
the amorality and immorality around me,
teach me that I am in this world,
though not a part of it.
Guide me in thinking through
the issues of my time,
not to grovel in the dirt,
but to have an awareness of need,
an understanding of truth,
and a willingness to respond with wisdom.
Lift my horizons, Jesus,
giving me a larger vision of my world
and my responsibilities within it.

TO ALL THE WORLD

"Listen! I have given you authority, so that you can walk on snakes and scorpions and overcome all the power of the Enemy, and nothing will hurt you. But don't be glad because the evil spirits obey you, rather be glad because your names are written in heaven."
(Luke 10:19-20)

Thank you for joy, Lord—
that soaring sense
that I can leap tall buildings,
walk on water,
or maybe even fly without a plane.
I praise you, Lord,
for the sense of expectancy
that you give me,
for the signs that follow,
as I say to all the world
that you are Lord!

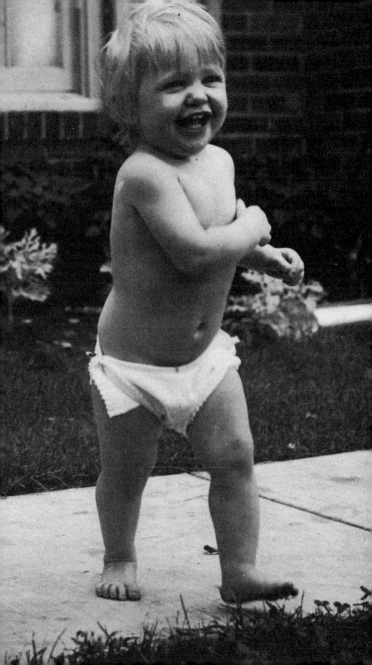

VALUED MOMENTS

I know that I will live to see the Lord's goodness in this present life (Ps. 27:13).

Too often I wait with building memories
until they must of necessity
become memorials.
Help me, Lord, to create moments
of joy or tenderness,
of laughter or quick response,
of listening or willingness to talk—
moments as valued as drops of dew
because they vanish as quickly.

TO BE CONFIDENT

"Remember that I have commanded you to be
determined and confident! Do not be afraid or
discouraged, for I, the Lord your God, am with you
wherever you go" (Josh. 1:9).

Sometimes I'm shaky
on the inside
because of wars,
rumors of wars,
catastrophic weather,
tragedies, or disease.
Yet remind me, Lord,
that fears limit me
and your faith strengthens.
Thank you for telling me
to not be afraid—even more,
for commanding me
to be confident
because of your presence.
Give me boldness
in repeating your promises
until your words
become mine through faith.
I *will* to trust you;
by the power of your Spirit
make it possible
for me to do so.

ABOUT FAILURE

I consider everything a loss compared to the surpassing
greatness of knowing Christ Jesus my Lord, for whose
sake I have lost all things. I consider them rubbish,
that I may gain Christ and be found in him, not having
a righteousness of my own that comes from the law, but
that which is through faith in Christ—the righteousness
that comes from God and is by faith (Phil. 3:8-9 NIV).

It seems I spend my life in being average,
or even worse, in less than average.
When my best attempts end in seeming failure,
help me remember, Jesus,
that from the viewpoint of the majority
you weren't so successful either.
Yet in your quiet way you loved
and brought wholeness
to every person receptive to you.
Thank you that I don't have to succeed,
if that success is measured against values
that are not yours. When my defeats—
or even the samenesses of my days—
threaten to overwhelm me,
renew your presence within me.
I praise you! I rejoice that I can count
all things worthless
in comparison with the joy of knowing you.

FRESHLY-DRAWN WATER

"Whoever drinks the water that I will give him will never be thirsty again. The water that I will give him will become in him a spring which will provide him with life-giving water and give him eternal life" (John 4:14).

Jesus, so often you come to me
as you came to the Samaritan woman,
offering life-giving water,
and I answer, "You don't have a bucket,
and the well is deep."
Always I forget that though you were man,
tempted as I am tempted,
yet you are also God.

Forgive me, Jesus, for listening to skeptics,
allowing them to wash away your cleansing hope.
Forgive me for looking at myself,
for seeing only inadequacies,
and believing that you function
out of the same desert that I do.
Forgive me for trying to understand your power,
rather than letting myself experience it.

Flow through me, Jesus, creating the knowledge
that with you nothing is impossible.
More than that, create in me the belief.

PENTECOST

*He gave them this command: "Do not leave Jerusalem,
but wait for the gift my Father promised, which you
have heard me speak about. For John baptized with
water, but in a few days you will be baptized with the
Holy Spirit. . . . But you will receive power when the
Holy Spirit comes to you; and you will be my witnesses
in Jerusalem, and in all Judea and Samaria, and to the
ends of the earth"* (Acts 1:4-5, 8 NIV).

Your disciples, Peter and John,
were told not to speak or teach in your name,
yet they answered, "We cannot stop speaking
of what we ourselves have seen and heard."
Why don't I feel that way?
Sometimes I'm afraid to even mention you,
but who am I serving—you?
Or those of whom I'm afraid?

Forgive my false assurance
in thinking I can witness and work
without the resource you have offered.
Take complete control, Jesus,
releasing in me the power of your Spirit.
Thank you for all you're going to do in my life,
using my full potential for your glory.

YOU'RE RIGHT!

I call to the Lord for help;
I plead with him.
I bring him all my complaints;
I tell him all my troubles.
When I am ready to give up,
he knows what I should do (Ps. 142:1-3).

Praise God!
There I was,
complaining again—
"This hasn't happened,
that hasn't changed,
this frustrates me,
that bothers me."
Then you reminded me
that you are Lord
over the frustrations
in my life,
and that I don't have
much to complain about
if I give everything
to you.
You're right!
Thank you, God.

EITHER WAY, I WIN

None of us lives for himself only, none of us dies for himself only. If we live, it is for the Lord that we live, and if we die, it is for the Lord that we die. So whether we live or die, we belong to the Lord.
(Rom. 14:7-8)

Thank you, Lord,
for making it possible
for me to believe
that either way, I win—
in facing death or facing life.
I praise you
for making me a winner,
whichever way the answer comes.
I rejoice that I am yours,
no matter what happens to me.

I want to live!
But you have freed me to live
by making me ready to die.
Thank you, Lord,
that whether I live or die,
I belong to you.
Thank you that eternal life
begins right now.

OUTSIDE THE TOMB OF LAZARUS

Then Mary, when she came where Jesus was and saw him, fell at his feet, saying to him, "Lord, if you had been here, my brother would not have died." When Jesus saw her weeping, and the Jews who came with her also weeping, he was deeply moved in spirit and troubled. . . . Jesus said to her, "Did I not tell you that if you would believe you would see the glory of God?" (John 11:32-33, 40 RSV)

Lord, it's only when I experience
disillusionment, suffering,
and the death of loved ones
that I begin to understand
the depth of your compassion.
Yet do you weep just for my pain,
or for the unbelief that lies beneath?
Forgive me, Lord.
Forgive my failure to believe
that *in everything* you act.
I praise you
that in your own time you come,
providing a better answer
after walking, and waiting, and weeping.

AN ALLELUIA

But let all who take refuge in you be glad;
let them ever sing for joy.
Spread your protection over them,
that those who love your name may rejoice in you.
(Ps. 5:11 NIV)

Lord, you have given me
a new song to sing!
Though the time ahead
stretches into the unknown,
I go forward filled with hope,
knowing you conduct the symphony
of the present and the future.
In my body, soul, and spirit,
you composed a melody;
in the discords of my life
you brought harmony.
I rejoice, Lord, I praise you!
Make me an alleluia
of your redeeming grace,
your everlasting love,
your overcoming power.